Carson-Dellosa Publishing

The Four-Blocks®
Literacy Model

Making Alphabet Books
to Teach Letters and Sounds

by
Dorothy P. Hall

Editors
Joey Bland
Tracy Soles

Artists
Courtney Bunn
Bill Neville

Cover Design
Jennifer Collins

With thanks and appreciation to my daughter, Michelle S. Hall, who teaches a kindergarten class for four-year-olds in the Bright Beginnings program at Plaza Road Prekindergarten, a Title 1 school in Charlotte, NC. Michelle shared the names of her students and helped me make sure that even four-year-olds could understand the words we were including in this book.

ISBN 0-88724-694-X

Table of Contents

Tongue Twisters, Names, and Predictable Charts

Introduction

Learning about letters and sounds has always been a part of beginning reading instruction. At one time, this meant workbooks and worksheets; and for some people, this may still be true. The past three decades have taught us much about how young children learn. We now know that workbooks and worksheets are not the best way! Early childhood specialists tell us that young children are active learners. When teachers use workbooks and worksheets, they are not allowing young children to learn by "doing." Workbooks and worksheets do not really teach—they are assessment instruments. They assess if children can recognize letters and the sounds associated with the letters. These pencil-and-paper tasks are too easy for some children, and are thus boring to them. For other children, these tasks are too difficult, and are thus frustrating to them. There are, however, activities that are "multilevel," meaning there is something to be gained by everyone in the class. These activities include the use of tongue twisters, names, and predictable charts. They help some children learn about letters and sounds while providing opportunities for other children to learn more about reading and writing, regardless of their literacy levels. For more information, please see *Month-by-Month Reading and Writing for Kindergarten* (Hall and Cunningham, 1997), *The Teacher's Guide to Building Blocks* (Hall and Williams, 2000), and *Predictable Charts* (Hall and Williams, 2001).

In this book, 26 letters and 35 sounds are introduced. The goal is to show young children that some letters make only one sound, while other letters are represented by two or more sounds. Thus, each sound will have its own tongue twister and predictable chart—the vowels with their "long" and "short" sounds; *c* and *g* with their "hard" and "soft" sounds; and two-letter combinations or digraphs that, when put together, do not blend their sounds together (like *bl*, *cr*, *st*, etc.) but come up with whole new sounds: *ch*, *sh*, and *th*. This method of showing children that some letters make more than one sound is a little different from traditional phonics, but also a little easier for children to understand. This is especially true when Cindy and Chad are listening to the "hard C" sound in cat and car, and wondering why their names start with the same letter but not with the same sound.

To make the alphabet books described in this text, children will be listening for sounds that begin alike in tongue twisters, looking for letters that make these sounds, using their names and the names of the other children in the class to add to the list of words, and finally, writing and reading predictable charts with these letters and sounds. The children can also make their own take-home alphabet books using the reproducible patterns from pages 54-90. More importantly, the children will be actively listening, looking, thinking, and reading, not just merely putting pencil or crayon to paper. I believe learning should be exciting and fun for both the children and their teacher, and I have watched teachers and children alike have fun with these activities. Do teachers need to teach these letters and sounds in isolation? No, but they often do it because that is how it traditionally has been done, not because it needs to be done this way. So, I have tried to combine what we have to do (teach letters and sounds) with some activities from which all children can benefit, regardless of their entering literacy levels.

Remember, there is no correct order in which to introduce letters and sounds. If your school or school system follows a basal or phonics program, use that order to introduce your tongue twisters and make your books. If you have no special order, then begin with the letters that make just one sound and are at the beginning of your students' names. Next, do the consonants that have more than one sound (*c* and *g*), then the vowels (which definitely have more than one sound, depending on what letters are near the vowel). Finally, do the letters that change sounds when two are together—the digraphs (*ch*, *sh*, and *th*). If you have children whose names begin with the chosen letter, then substitute their names in the tongue twister. If you don't have any children in your classroom whose names begin with that letter, then simply use the tongue twister as it is written. **If you have Hispanic children in your class and their names begin with the letter *J*, then you may have to add the H sound for *J* because that is common in Spanish.**

Why Use Tongue Twisters?

Tongue Twisters give examples of words that begin with the same sound and are fun for children to say. They are said slowly the first time, and then after several attempts, children can say them easily and a little (or a lot!) faster. Tongue twisters are also a link between phonemic awareness (hearing phonemes or "sounds" in words—the oral) and phonics (knowing which letters make which sounds—the visual).

David and Dominique dance with Dalmatians.

Phonemic awareness is the awareness that words are composed of sounds, and it is an important precursor of learning to read (Yopp, 1992). Phonemic awareness is the oral before the written. It is the ability to hear the phonemes (sounds) in words that letters make. A child that has phonemic awareness can tell you that Michelle, mommy, and McDonald's® all begin with the same sound. They may not know that the words begin with the letter *M* or what sound the letter *M* makes at the beginning of a word, but they can hear the same sound at the beginning of each of the three familiar words. Before the 1990s, educators did not talk about phonemic awareness, and teachers did not worry about teaching it. Then, educators of young children began to teach phonics as soon as children entered school. Phonics was a skill that schools taught in first grade, but then soon it crept into kindergarten and pre-kindergarten. Sometimes, children were even asked to master phonics before they were allowed to learn to read in first grade!

According to Adams (1991) and Cunningham and Allington (2001), only 40 to 50 percent of children come to school with sufficient phonemic awareness. When children lack phonemic awareness, they are not ready to learn about letters and sounds. They are also not ready for what we traditionally call phonics instruction. Phonemic awareness is the best predictor of success in learning to read. When the importance of phonemic awareness was recognized, schools began to stress this with their young students. The difference between phonics and phonemic awareness was often unknown, and sometimes old phonics materials were repackaged as phonemic awareness materials, adding to the confusion of educators.

Tongue twisters, like *Jolly Jimmy jumps for joy in January.* (Hall and Cunningham, 1997), help develop phonemic awareness. As children listen for the sounds they hear at the beginning of many of the words (*Jolly, Jimmy, jumps, joy, January*), their brains become pattern detectors. First, the children listen to the tongue twister and then say it. Once they hear that many of the words begin with the same sound, they are ready to see what letter is making that sound. As they look at the tongue twister, they see the same beginning letter (*J-j*) in these words. Tongue twisters help link phonemic awareness (the oral) and phonics (the written). When working with tongue twisters, the teacher then asks, "Does anyone have a name that begins with that sound?" She repeats the names as she writes them on the board or a piece of chart paper. Then, the teacher asks, "Does anyone know any other words that begin with that sound?"

This is where phonics instruction used to begin, with the teacher asking for words that begin with a certain sound (*J*). We now know all children can participate if we start with a tongue twister (the oral first), look at the letter that makes the sound in the words that begin alike, talk about names we know that begin with that sound, and then go to other words that begin with the letter sound on which we are focusing. If children cannot hear the letter that is the same in each tongue twister, then there is no need to look at letters or to talk about what letter makes that sound! If children can't hear that words begin alike, they are not ready for phonics. Many of the tongue twisters in this book are also "action phonics." The children can "act out" these tongue twisters (*Jeremy and Jazmin jiggle like jelly.*), giving them one more memory aid.

Why Use Children's Names?

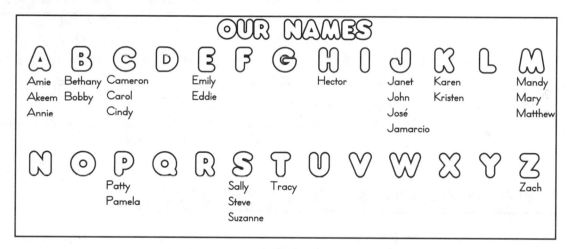

Names are interesting to children—especially their own and those of their classmates! Names are something to which most children can connect letters and sounds. Brain research tells us that children have trouble remembering information unless they can connect that information to something they already know. There are two types of learning based on the brain's two types of memory stores. Tasks we do "over and over again" until we learn them are put into the rote memory store. This rote memory has a limited capacity, and if we do not practice something that is in the rote memory store, that space is given over to something that is more current. To illustrate this, just think of all the things you learned in geometry, chemistry, physics, and even statistics that are now long forgotten!

The other memory store is the associative memory store. It has an unlimited capacity. Things in the associative memory that have not been used for years can be recalled when triggered by the right image, smell, song, name, etc. The trick of putting things into the associative, rather than the rote, memory store is to make associations or "connections" with the information. Some young children who are trying to learn what a letter is, and that a line made with a certain shape is called a *j*, and that this *j* has a certain sound, simply cannot remember this much information. Often, when young children are asked, "What letter does that begin with?" they cannot give the teacher the correct letter name. Ask instead, "Whose name starts with that sound or letter?" and you will get a different response. Why? The children can remember the information if they can connect this letter and sound to some "interesting-to-them" words—and names make a natural connection.

My daughter Michelle teaches a kindergarten class for four-year-olds at a Title I School in Charlotte, NC. She tells me that her students can tell whose name "starts like that" long before they know all the letter names and sounds. Names are important and meaningful for young children. If you can use the names of children in your class for these tongue twisters and predictable charts, then use them. If you have Johnny and Jennifer in your class, it is much more powerful to use their names in the *J-j* tongue twister, rather than the names provided in the text. It is also important to talk about all the names the children know that begin with that sound. Let them tell you, "My dad's name is Joey." or "My other name is Johnson." These responses show that the children are listening and linking the sound on which you are focusing to other sounds in words they know.

Why Make Predictable Charts and Class Alphabet Books?

D is for...
D is for David. (Mrs. Davis)
D is for Daniel. (Daniel)
D is for dog. (Amy)
D is for doll. (Cindy)
D is for duck. (Susie)
D is for draw. (Joseph)

"Predictable Charts" is the new name given by Pat Cunningham to an idea she first wrote about in 1979 and called "structured language experience." Pat has told me that we didn't have predictable books at that time, so naming this as predictable charts did not occur to her. As soon as "predictable big books" and later "predictable little books" appeared in primary classrooms, she realized that "structured language experience" charts were really "predictable charts."

For those teachers too young to remember, language experience was a popular way to teach beginning reading in the 1970s. The philosophy behind the language experience approach was that if you could say a sentence ("I went to the mall."), you could write it, and if the sentence written down was the child's words, then the child could probably read it. The problem with language experience was that some children entered school without being able to talk in complete sentences. These children could not take part in this early reading/writing activity. If the teacher wrote a complete sentence instead of the children's words (an incomplete sentence), then the children could not read it back because it was not really "their words." So, these children could not take part in language experience activities, and they were the very children who needed these early reading/writing activities most. It occurred to Pat Cunningham that if the sentences were structured (I can..., I saw..., I am thankful for..., etc.), all children could take part in these activities. Few teachers read her article on this subject, since it appeared in an obscure journal, but Pat also taught the concept to her graduate and undergraduate students. Those that tried this activity found that all students not only could take part, they also could experience success with beginning reading and writing.

Making predictable charts based on the alphabet is a multilevel activity. Some students will be able to read the entire chart, and thus, the entire class alphabet book. Other children can read their sentences, and then can read their own pages when the book is made, and perhaps a few other pages as well. They notice that all the sentences start alike and could probably read the start of each sentence if asked. Still other young children are only able to read their own sentences, but they notice that the teacher goes from left to right and top to bottom as she writes the chart. Because the class dictated the sentences that are written on the chart, and made the sentences into a book, the children know what the book is about. Many children will be able to "pretend" read this book using the structure of the text and the illustrations when they pick up this book in the classroom reading center.

The Five-Day Cycle for Predictable Charts

Most predictable charts are made into class big books with teachers following a five-day cycle of literacy activities. The five-day cycle would look like this:

Day 1: Tongue Twister and Sentence Dictation

- First, the teacher reads the tongue twister with the letter sound on which she wants the children to focus for the week.

- Next, the teacher repeats the tongue twister and asks the children to listen for a sound they hear at the beginning of many of the words. She calls on children to tell her words they heard with this beginning sound. The teacher asks the children to look at the tongue twister and see if they can find the letter that is making that sound. Then, the teacher asks the children, "Do you know any names that begin like this?" After the children tell her the names they know which begin with that sound, she asks, "Do you know any other words that begin like this?"

- Finally, the teacher begins a predictable chart on a large piece of lined paper by giving the children a model sentence or pattern to follow: "J is for juice." She writes her name in parentheses after the sentence (Mrs. Hall). Then, the children dictate their own sentences, using the model given, and the teacher writes each sentence on the chart paper, putting the children's names in parentheses at the end.

J is for...
J is for juice. (Mrs. Hall)
J is for jelly. (Latrell)
J is for Jackie. (Maura)
J is for jump. (Jenny)
J is for Joey. (Robbie)
J is for jump rope. (Lisa)

Day 2: Tongue Twister and Sentence Dictation (Continued)

The teacher reads the tongue twister again, and then reads all the sentences written on the *J-j* chart so far, touching each of the words as she reads them. The teacher asks the remainder of the children for a sentence and completes the predictable chart for the letter *J-j*.

Day 3: "Touch Reading" the Sentences

The teacher asks the students to "touch read" the sentences they dictated for the chart. She models this for the children by touch reading her sentence—reading the sentence aloud and touching each word as she reads it. At this time, it is helpful to move the chart to the students' eye level, so each child can easily read his sentence and touch the words. By touching each word as they read their sentences, many of the children will learn to track print.

Day 4: Sentence Builders

The teacher focuses on the sentences, each of the words in the sentences, and the sounds of the letters with an activity called "sentence builders." Before the lesson, the teacher writes three or four sentences from the predictable chart onto sentence strips. She includes the name of the child who dictated the sentence. Next, the teacher cuts the words apart and puts them in an envelope or clear plastic bag. Using one sentence at a time, the teacher passes out the words to as many children as she has words, giving the name in parentheses to the child whose sentence is being built. The students are then asked to be "sentence builders" and "build the sentence" by putting the words in the same order as they are in the sentence written on the chart. When the children have done this, the teacher stands behind the sentence builders and touches each child on the head or shoulder as she reads the words in the sentence with the class. She repeats this process for the other cut-apart sentences.

Day 5: Making the Class Book

- Before the final day's activity, the teacher writes all the sentences from the chart on sentence strips and cuts them apart into words. She begins the lesson by letting the children read their sentences again from the chart, one sentence at a time.

- After reading the chart, the teacher models gluing her sentence on a blank piece of paper and talks about the picture she will draw above it. Then, she gives the children their cut-apart sentences and asks them to put the words in their sentences in the correct order. Tell the children to check their sentences with you before they begin gluing. (This prevents the mess of having the words glued in the wrong order!) These papers will serve as the "pages" for the class book.

- The children can then illustrate their sentences in the space above the pasted words. If you begin this activity early in the school year, when many students will have difficulty putting their sentences in order, simply write each child's sentence on the bottom of a blank sheet of paper instead of on the sentence strip. After several weeks of doing this activity, the children will be able to put the words in their sentences in order and paste them down.

- Finally, the teacher makes the book cover and staples or binds the pages together. Now the students have a class big book to treasure and read all year!

As the year progresses and the class makes more alphabet books, the teacher continues to write the sentences on sentence strips, but gives the sentence strips to the students to cut apart into words. She may also mix up the words in each sentence when writing them so that the student not only has to cut the words apart, but also rearrange the words in the correct order. Another more challenging task for the children is to let them copy the sentences for the class book from the chart. With this activity, the students are not only learning about letters and sounds, but also learning more about reading and writing and working independently. Give the children who can do these tasks the opportunity, but remember to continue to support and help those children who are not ready for the tasks.

Summary of the Five-Day Cycle

Day 1

Read the tongue twister to the class and:

• ask the children to listen for words that start alike

• ask the children to look at the letter that begins those words

• ask for names that begin with that letter and sound

• ask for other words that begin with the same sound

Begin a predictable chart by modeling the first sentence, then have the children dictate sentences of their own.

Day 2

Have the rest of the children dictate their sentences.

Day 3

Have each child touch read his sentence.

Day 4

Cut the chart into strips and give each child his strip. Have each child cut his strip into words, reassemble and glue it on a large piece of paper, and then illustrate it.

Day 5

The children's completed papers are combined into a class book, and children make a take-home book of the letter.

Making Take-Home Alphabet Books

If you are going to use the take-home alphabet book patterns from pages 54-90, then combine the steps from Days 4 and 5, and make the individual alphabet books on Day 5. Many teachers want students to have their own little books—something they can make, take home, and keep. When folded, the pattern becomes a "book" with pages for names/words that begin with that letter sound. The teacher makes copies of the selected pattern, folds the pages along the dotted lines, and passes the books out to the class. The children sit at their desks, read the tongue twister on the cover together, then color the illustration. Next, the children decide which names or words they want to add to their pages. They draw the chosen pictures, one on each page, or they can write the word and draw the picture (depending on the time of year) to complete their individual alphabet books.

In order to make this activity even more multilevel, preschool children can simply draw a picture on each page of their take-home books. Kindergartners can draw a picture and try their hand at labeling their illustrations, as well. First graders can choose to make the simple four-page individual alphabet books by following the patterns with pictures and sentence starters on pages 54-89. Challenge your first graders to take it a step further by cutting the folds at the top of the simple book pattern after it is folded to make an eight-page book. Once the cuts are made, add two staples to the left side of the book and have your students write the appropriate sentence starter on the extra pages.

Why Write This Book?

Elaine Williams, a wonderful kindergarten teacher, and I wrote a book together called *Predictable Charts* (Hall and Williams, 2001). The book was so well-received by kindergarten and first-grade teachers that soon after it was written, I began to think of a sequel. The idea of making alphabet books to learn about letters and sounds and using tongue twisters, names, and predictable charts came to me while I was teaching in a half-day kindergarten class at Lew Wallace Elementary School in Hammond, Indiana.

I did a morning message first, and then, since it was January, I did a *J* tongue twister from *Month-by-Month Reading and Writing for Kindergarten* (Hall and Cunningham, 1997), *"Jolly Jimmy jumps for joy in January."* I wrote this tongue twister after my morning message. We listened for the words that started alike (*Jolly, Jimmy, jumps, joy, January*), and then looked at those words. We talked about the sounds we heard and the letter we saw—*J-j.* Then I asked, "Does anyone have a name that begins like *Jimmy*?" To my surprise, four children (Jackie, Jazmin, Johnny, and James) raised their hands, along with a boy whose father's name was Joey and someone else whose last name was Johnson. The children listened as I repeated the names and started a list of names that begin with *J*. I told them I knew some other words that began with that sound: *jam*, *jump*, and *jelly*. Then, the children told me some words they knew: *jump rope*, *juice*, *jeep*, and *jewelry*. Next, we began writing a predictable chart. I took the lead and modeled the first sentence by saying, "J is for juice." and wrote the letters and words as I said them. I called on the children individually, and as each one said a sentence, I wrote the words as I repeated it aloud. I placed the child's name in parentheses at the end of the sentence as I said his name.

Here is what our chart looked like:

J is for...
J is for juice. (Mrs. Hall)
J is for jelly. (Latrell)
J is for Jackie. (Maura)
J is for jump. (Jenny)
J is for Joey. (Robbie)
J is for jump rope. (Lisa)

When we were finished, we read the chart together. I wrote two of their sentences on sentence strips, cut the words apart, and then had the children become "sentence builders." I gave each word from one of the sentences to five different children. "J" went to one child, "is" to a second child, "for" to a third child, the name "Jackie" to a fourth child, and since it was Maura's sentence, she got the part of the strip that had her name in parentheses "(Maura)." I asked the children to "build" the sentence from the chart by lining themselves up in the right order. When the five students had their sentence built, I touched their heads as we read the sentence aloud, "J is for Jackie. (Maura)." Then, we did sentence builders with a second sentence.

The success (and fun!) these kindergarten children had with these activities convinced me that Elaine and I had left out an important kind of predictable chart when we wrote the *Predictable Charts* book. The purpose of these predictable charts is to introduce, or review, all the letters and the sound(s) the letters make. If teachers want to do the "Letter of the Week," then this activity might be one way to do it so that all children can benefit, regardless of their literacy levels. The purpose of this book and these predictable charts is to introduce, or review, all the letters and sounds these letters make.

A Note about Alphabet Books

Alphabet books help children grow in phonemic awareness, and there are many on the market today. The best ones for young children are those with just a word or two, or a sentence, on the page; too much print on the page can be a problem for some emergent readers. There are a few simple alphabet books that have a tongue twister for each letter. Reading these to children helps them hear letters with the same sound in succession. Two of my favorites are *Animalia* by Graeme Base and *ABCD: An Alphabet Book of Cats and Dogs* by Sheila Moxley. For a more complete list of alphabet books, see pages 92-95.

A a

Amie and Asia ate apricots.

Day 1

Read the tongue twister to the class and:

- ask the children to listen for words that start alike
- ask the children to look at the letter that begins those words...........**A a**
- ask for names that begin with that letter and sound
  - **Amie**, **Abel**, **Asia**, **Adrian**
- ask for other words that begin with the same sound
  - **acorn**, **apron**, **ate**, **acre**

Begin a predictable chart by modeling the first sentence, then have the children dictate sentences of their own.

Day 2

Have the rest of the children dictate their sentences.

Day 3

Have each child touch read her sentence.

Day 4

Cut the chart into strips and give each child her strip. Have each child cut her strip into words, reassemble and glue it on a large piece of paper, and then illustrate it.

Day 5

The children's completed papers are combined into a class book, and children make take-home books of the letter.

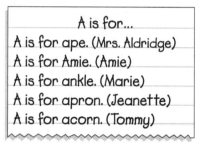

A is for acorn. (Tommy)

1. Copy.

2. Fold.

3. Take home.

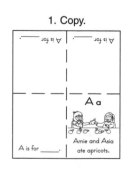

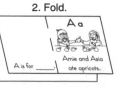

A a

Alex and Amber always avoid asparagus.

Day 1

Read the tongue twister to the class and:
- ask the children to listen for words that start alike
- ask the children to look at the letter that begins those words..........**A a**
- ask for names that begin with that letter and sound
  - **Akeem**, **Annie, Amber, Alexander**
- ask for other words that begin with the same sound
  - **ant, answer, ask, and, animal**

Begin a predictable chart by modeling the first sentence, then have the children dictate sentences of their own.

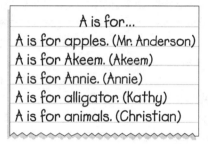

Day 2

Have the rest of the children dictate their sentences.

Day 3

Have each child touch read his sentence.

Day 4

Cut the chart into strips and give each child his strip. Have each child cut his strip into words, reassemble and glue it on a large piece of paper, and then illustrate it.

Day 5

The children's completed papers are combined into a class book, and children make take-home books of the letter.

A is for alligator. (Kathy)

A is for...

1. Copy.

2. Fold.

3. Take home.

B b

Brianna and Ben bounce beach balls.

Day 1

Read the tongue twister to the class and:
- ask the children to listen for words that start alike
- ask the children to look at the letter that begins those words...........**B b**
- ask for names that begin with that letter and sound
  - **Bobby**, **Bethany, Betsy, Brad**
- ask for other words that begin with the same sound
  - **ball, bat, boy, bean**

Begin a predictable chart by modeling the first sentence, then have the children dictate sentences of their own.

Day 2

Have the rest of the children dictate their sentences.

Day 3

Have each child touch read her sentence.

Day 4

Cut the chart into strips and give each child her strip. Have each child cut her strip into words, reassemble and glue it on a large piece of paper, and then illustrate it.

Day 5

The children's completed papers are combined into a class book, and children make take-home books of the letter.

B is for...
B is for baby. (Mrs. Marr)
B is for Bethany. (Bethany)
B is for Bobby. (Bobby)
B is for boat. (Will)
B is for balloon. (Joyce)

B is for...
B is for baby. (Mrs. Marr)
B is for Beth_y. (Bethany)
B is for Bob_
B is for boat. (W___
B is for balloon. (Joy__

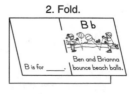

B is for boat. (Will)

B is for...

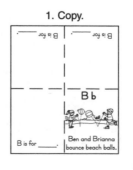

1. Copy.

B is for

B is for

B b

B is for _____   Ben and Brianna bounce beach balls.

2. Fold.

B b

B is for _____   Ben and Brianna bounce beach balls.

3. Take home.

B b

Ben and Brianna bounce beach balls.

C c

Carol and Caitlyn count candy corn.

Day 1

Read the tongue twister to the class and:
- ask the children to listen for words that start alike
- ask the children to look at the letter that begins those words...........**C c**
- ask for names that begin with that letter and sound
  - **Connie, Calvin, Carol, Caitlyn, Caleb**
- ask for other words that begin with the same sound
  - **cup, crow, cap, coat**

Begin a predictable chart by modeling the first sentence, then have the children dictate sentences of their own.

Day 2

Have the rest of the children dictate their sentences.

Day 3

Have each child touch read his sentence.

Day 4

Cut the chart into strips and give each child his strip. Have each child cut his strip into words, reassemble and glue it on a large piece of paper, and then illustrate it.

Day 5

The children's completed papers are combined into a class book, and children make take-home books of the letter.

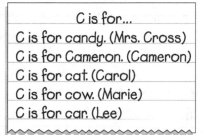

C is for...
C is for candy. (Mrs. Cross)
C is for Cameron. (Cameron)
C is for cat. (Carol)
C is for cow. (Marie)
C is for car. (Lee)

C is for cow. (Marie)

C is for...

1. Copy.

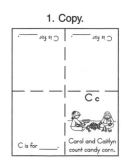

2. Fold.

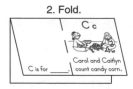

3. Take home.

C c

Cindy celebrates with cider and celery.

Day 1

Read the tongue twister to the class and:
- ask the children to listen for words that start alike
- ask the children to look at the letter that begins those words...........**C c**
- ask for names that begin with that letter and sound
  - **Cindy, Cecil, Cedrick, Cinderella**
- ask for other words that begin with the same sound
  - **cent, circus, cycle**

Begin a predictable chart by modeling the first sentence, then have the children dictate sentences of their own.

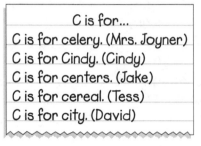

C is for...
C is for celery. (Mrs. Joyner)
C is for Cindy. (Cindy)
C is for centers. (Jake)
C is for cereal. (Tess)
C is for city. (David)

Day 2

Have the rest of the children dictate their sentences.

Day 3

Have each child touch read her sentence.

C is for...
C is for celery. (Mrs. Joyn
C is for Cind (Cindy)
C is for cen   ke)
C is for cereal. (
C is for city. (David)

Day 4

Cut the chart into strips and give each child her strip. Have each child cut her strip into words, reassemble and glue it on a large piece of paper, and then illustrate it.

Day 5

The children's completed papers are combined into a class book, and children make take-home books of the letter.

C is for cereal. (Tess)

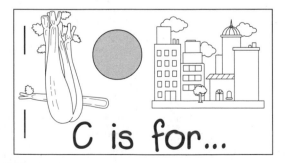

C is for...

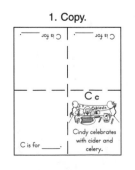

1. Copy.

C is for

2. Fold.

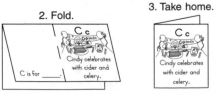

C is for _____.

3. Take home.

C c
Cindy celebrates with cider and celery.

Ch ch

Chad and Chip chew cherries and chocolate.

Day 1

Read the tongue twister to the class and:
- ask the children to listen for words that start alike
- ask the children to look at the letters that begin those words...........**Ch ch**
- ask for names that begin with the letters and sound
  - **Chastity, Chad, Chelsea, Chip**
- ask for other words that begin with the same sound
  - **cheer, chin, chart, chimp**

Begin a predictable chart by modeling the first sentence, then have the children dictate sentences of their own.

Day 2

Have the rest of the children dictate their sentences.

Day 3

Have each child touch read his sentence.

Day 4

Cut the chart into strips and give each child his strip. Have each child cut his strip into words, reassemble and glue it on a large piece of paper, and then illustrate it.

Day 5

The children's completed papers are combined into a class book, and children make take-home books of the sound.

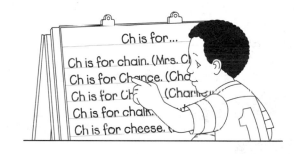

Ch is for...
Ch is for chain. (Mrs. Charles)
Ch is for Chance. (Chance)
Ch is for Charlie. (Charlie)
Ch is for chalk. (Hoyt)
Ch is for cheese. (Britta)

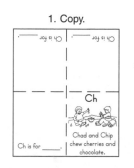

Ch is for chalk. (Hoyt)

Ch is for...

1. Copy.

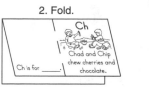

2. Fold.

3. Take home.

D d

David and Dominique dance with Dalmatians.

Day 1

Read the tongue twister to the class and:
- ask the children to listen for words that start alike
- ask the children to look at the letter that begins those words...........**D d**
- ask for names that begin with that letter and sound
  - **Dominique, David, Deidre, Dorothy, Dexter**
- ask for other words that begin with the same sound
  - **dog, day, door, doll, dolphin**

Begin a predictable chart by modeling the first sentence, then have the children dictate sentences of their own.

Day 2

Have the rest of the children dictate their sentences.

Day 3

Have each child touch read her sentence.

Day 4

Cut the chart into strips and give each child her strip. Have each child cut her strip into words, reassemble and glue it on a large piece of paper, and then illustrate it.

Day 5

The children's completed papers are combined into a class book, and children make take-home books of the letter.

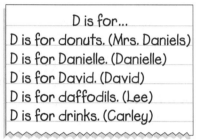

D is for...
D is for donuts. (Mrs. Daniels)
D is for Danielle. (Danielle)
D is for David. (David)
D is for daffodils. (Lee)
D is for drinks. (Carley)

D is for...
D is for donuts. (Mrs. Dani
D is for Dar   (Danielle)
D is for Dav
D is for daffodil
D is for drinks. (Carley

D is for dog. (Sarah)

D is for...

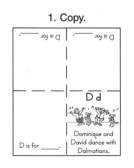

1. Copy.

D is for ___

Dominique and David dance with Dalmatians.

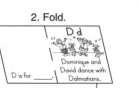

2. Fold.

D d

Dominique and David dance with Dalmatians.

D is for ___

3. Take home.

D d

Dominique and David dance with Dalmatians.

24

E e

Elizabeth and Ethan eat eclairs.

Day 1

Read the tongue twister to the class and:
- ask the children to listen for words that start alike
- ask the children to look at the letter that begins those words...........**E e**
- ask for names that begin with that letter and sound
  - **Emilio, Ethan, Eve, Elijah, Elaine**
- ask for other words that begin with the same sound
  - **easel, equal, even, evil**

Begin a predictable chart by modeling the first sentence, then have the children dictate sentences of their own.

Day 2

Have the rest of the children dictate their sentences.

Day 3

Have each child touch read his sentence.

Day 4

Cut the chart into strips and give each child his strip. Have each child cut his strip into words, reassemble and glue it on a large piece of paper, and then illustrate it.

Day 5

The children's completed papers are combined into a class book, and children make take-home books of the letter.

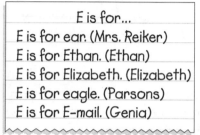

E is for...
E is for ear. (Mrs. Reiker)
E is for Ethan. (Ethan)
E is for Elizabeth. (Elizabeth)
E is for eagle. (Parsons)
E is for E-mail. (Genia)

E is for eagle. (Parsons)

E is for...

1. Copy.

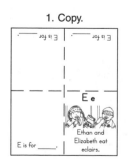

2. Fold.

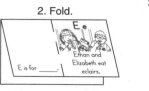

3. Take home.

E e

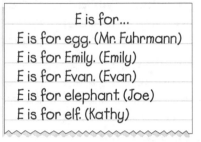

Emily and Eddie enjoy eggs.

Day 1

Read the tongue twister to the class and:
- ask the children to listen for words that start alike
- ask the children to look at the letter that begins those words..........**E e**
- ask for names that begin with that letter and sound
  - **Erin, Elmo, Eric, Ellen, Emily**
- ask for other words that begin with the same sound
  - **end, edge, elbow**

Begin a predictable chart by modeling the first sentence, then have the children dictate sentences of their own.

Day 2

Have the rest of the children dictate their sentences.

Day 3

Have each child touch read her sentence.

Day 4

Cut the chart into strips and give each child her strip. Have each child cut her strip into words, reassemble and glue it on a large piece of paper, and then illustrate it.

Day 5

The children's completed papers are combined into a class book, and children make take-home books of the letter.

E is for...
E is for egg. (Mr. Fuhrmann)
E is for Emily. (Emily)
E is for Evan. (Evan)
E is for elephant. (Joe)
E is for elf. (Kathy)

E is for elf. (Kathy)

E is for...

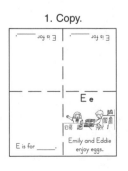

1. Copy.

E is for ___.

E e

Emily and Eddie enjoy eggs.

E is for ___

2. Fold.

E e

E is for ___

Emily and Eddie enjoy eggs.

3. Take home.

E e

Emily and Eddie enjoy eggs.

26

F f

Felicia and Freddy follow funny footprints.

Day 1

Read the tongue twister to the class and:
- ask the children to listen for words that start alike
- ask the children to look at the letter that begins those words...........**F f**
- ask for names that begin with that letter and sound
  - **Faith, Felipe, Frances, Frank**
- ask for other words that begin with the same sound
  - **food, face, four, fan, foot**

Begin a predictable chart by modeling the first sentence, then have the children dictate sentences of their own.

Day 2

Have the rest of the children dictate their sentences.

Day 3

Have each child touch read his sentence.

Day 4

Cut the chart into strips and give each child his strip. Have each child cut his strip into words, reassemble and glue it on a large piece of paper, and then illustrate it.

Day 5

The children's completed papers are combined into a class book, and children make take-home books of the letter.

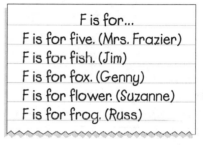

F is for...
F is for five. (Mrs. Frazier)
F is for fish. (Jim)
F is for fox. (Genny)
F is for flower. (Suzanne)
F is for frog. (Russ)

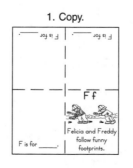

F is for flower. (Suzanne)

F is for...

1. Copy.

2. Fold.

3. Take home.

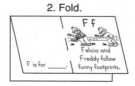

G g

Gail and Gwen grow goodies in their garden.

Day 1

Read the tongue twister to the class and:
- ask the children to listen for words that start alike
- ask the children to look at the letter that begins those words...........**G g**
- ask for names that begin with that letter and sound
  - **Gabrielle, Gilbert, Guillermo, Gloria**
- ask for other words that begin with the same sound
  - **girl, gum, go, good**

Begin a predictable chart by modeling the first sentence, then have the children dictate sentences of their own.

Day 2

Have the rest of the children dictate their sentences.

Day 3

Have each child touch read her sentence.

Day 4

Cut the chart into strips and give each child her strip. Have each child cut her strip into words, reassemble and glue it on a large piece of paper, and then illustrate it.

Day 5

The children's completed papers are combined into a class book, and children make take-home books of the letter.

G is for...
G is for Gail. (Mrs. Gibson)
G is for game. (Terry)
G is for goat. (G.W.)
G is for garden. (Matthew)
G is for guesses. (William)

G is for game. (Terry)

G is for...

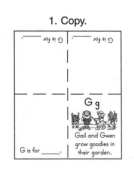

1. Copy.

G is for _____.

2. Fold.

3. Take home.

G g

Ginger and George like giraffes and gerbils.

Day 1

Reads the tongue twister to the class and:
- ask the children to listen for words that start alike
- ask the children to look at the letter that begins those words...........**G g**
- ask for names that begin with that letter and sound
  - **Gene, Gerald, Gina, Geraldine**
- ask for other words that begin with the same sound
  - **giant, gym, germ, gerbil**

Begin a predictable chart by modeling the first sentence, then have the children dictate sentences of their own.

Day 2

Have the rest of the children dictate their sentences.

Day 3

Have each child touch read his sentence.

Day 4

Cut the chart into strips and give each child his strip. Have each child cut his strip into words, reassemble and glue it on a large piece of paper, and then illustrate it.

Day 5

The children's completed papers are combined into a class book, and children make take-home books of the letter.

G is for...
G is for Ginger. (Mrs. Gingras)
G is for George. (Billy)
G is for gingerbread. (Karen)
G is for gem. (Matthew)
G is for gerbil. (Kristen)

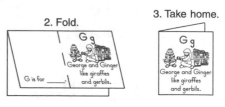

G is for gingerbread. (Karen)

G is for...

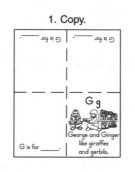

1. Copy.

2. Fold.

3. Take home.

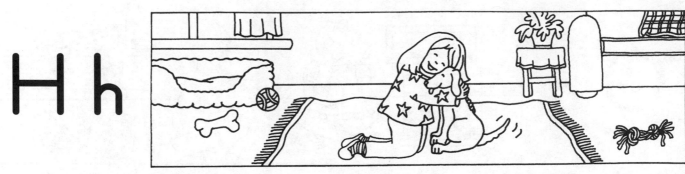

H h

Hannah hugs Harry the happy hound.

Day 1

Read the tongue twister to the class and:
- ask the children to listen for words that start alike
- ask the children to look at the letter that begins those words...........**H h**
- ask for names that begin with that letter and sound
  - **Harriet, Hector, Hank, Heather, Horace**
- ask for other words that begin with the same sound
  - **hill, house, heart, he**

Begin a predictable chart by modeling the first sentence, then have the children dictate sentences of their own.

Day 2

Have the rest of the children dictate their sentences.

Day 3

Have each child touch read her sentence.

Day 4

Cut the chart into strips and give each child her strip. Have each child cut her strip into words, reassemble and glue it on a large piece of paper, and then illustrate it.

Day 5

The children's completed papers are combined into a class book, and children make take-home books of the letter.

H is for...
H is for Hector. (Mrs. Hall)
H is for hand. (Betty)
H is for hat. (Mickey)
H is for house. (Ben)
H is for helicopter. (Jason)

H is for hat. (Mickey)

H is for...

1. Copy.

H is for _____.

H h

Hannah hugs
Harry the happy
hound.

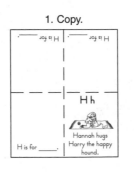

2. Fold.

H h

Hannah hugs
Harry the happy
hound.

H is for _____.

3. Take home.

H h

Hannah hugs
Harry the happy
hound.

I i

Isaac and Iris like ice cubes and ice cream.

Day 1

Read the tongue twister to the class and:
- ask the children to listen for words that start alike
- ask the children to look at the letter that begins those words..........**I i**
- ask for names that begin with that letter and sound
  - **Ivy, Ike, Inez, Ivan, Isiah**
- ask for other words that begin with the same sound
  - **I, ice, idea**

Begin a predictable chart by modeling the first sentence, then have the children dictate sentences of their own.

Day 2

Have the rest of the children dictate their sentences.

Day 3

Have each child touch read his sentence.

Day 4

Cut the chart into strips and give each child his strip. Have each child cut his strip into words, reassemble and glue it on a large piece of paper, and then illustrate it.

Day 5

The children's completed papers are combined into a class book, and children make take-home books of the letter.

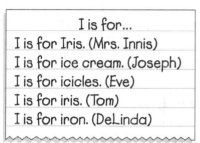

I is for...
I is for Iris. (Mrs. Innis)
I is for ice cream. (Joseph)
I is for icicles. (Eve)
I is for iris. (Tom)
I is for iron. (DeLinda)

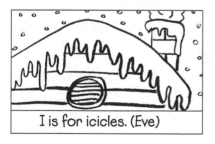

I is for icicles. (Eve)

I is for...

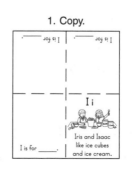

1. Copy.

2. Fold.

3. Take home.

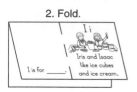

I i

Isadora and Iggie have inchworms that itch.

Day 1

Read the tongue twister to the class and:
- ask the children to listen for words that start alike
- ask the children to look at the letter that begins those words...........**I i**
- ask for names that begin with that letter and sound
  - **Isabel, Iggie, Imani, Israel, Ivana**
- ask for other words that begin with the same sound
  - **Internet, is, inside, imagination**

Begin a predictable chart by modeling the first sentence, then have the children dictate sentences of their own.

Day 2

Have the rest of the children dictate their sentences.

Day 3

Have each child touch read her sentence.

Day 4

Cut the chart into strips and give each child her strip. Have each child cut her strip into words, reassemble and glue it on a large piece of paper, and then illustrate it.

Day 5

The children's completed papers are combined into a class book, and children make take-home books of the letter.

I is for...
I is for Isabel. (Mr. Iccato)
I is for ink. (Jeannie)
I is for igloo. (Donnie)
I is for inch. (Christine)
I is for Internet. (Fran)

I is for...
I is for Isabel. (Mr. Iccato)
I is for ink. (Jannie)
I is for igloo. (Chr...)
I is for inch. (Chr...)
I is for Internet. (Fran)

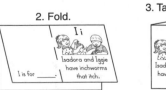

I is for ink. (Jeannie)

I is for...

1. Copy.

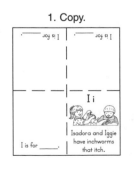

2. Fold.

3. Take home.

J j

Jeremy and Jazmin jiggle like jelly.

Day 1

Read the tongue twister to the class and:
- ask the children to listen for words that start alike
- ask the children to look at the letter that begins those words..........**J j**
- ask for names that begin with that letter and sound
  - **Jack, Judy, Joey, Janet, Jeff**
- ask for other words that begin with the same sound
  - **juice, jump, jet, job, jam**

Begin a predictable chart by modeling the first sentence, then have the children dictate sentences of their own.

Day 2

Have the rest of the children dictate their sentences.

Day 3

Have each child touch read his sentence.

Day 4

Cut the chart into strips and give each child his strip. Have each child cut his strip into words, reassemble and glue it on a large piece of paper, and then illustrate it.

Day 5

The children's completed papers are combined into a class book, and children make take-home books of the letter.

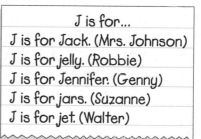

J is for...
J is for Jack. (Mrs. Johnson)
J is for jelly. (Robbie)
J is for Jennifer. (Genny)
J is for jars. (Suzanne)
J is for jet. (Walter)

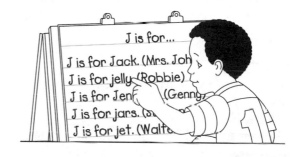

J is for jars. (Suzanne)

J is for...

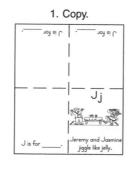

1. Copy.

2. Fold.

3. Take home.

K k

Kendall and Kiana kick like kangaroos.

Day 1

Read the tongue twister to the class and:
- ask the children to listen for words that start alike
- ask the children to look at the letter that begins those words...........**K k**
- ask for names that begin with that letter and sound
  - **Kelly, Kevin, Keith, Kimberly, Kanesha**
- ask for other words that begin with the same sound
  - **key, kid, kiss, kitten**

Begin a predictable chart by modeling the first sentence, then have the children dictate sentences of their own.

Day 2

Have the rest of the children dictate their sentences.

Day 3

Have each child touch read her sentence.

Day 4

Cut the chart into strips and give each child her strip. Have each child cut her strip into words, reassemble and glue it on a large piece of paper, and then illustrate it.

Day 5

The children's completed papers are combined into a class book, and children make take-home books of the letter.

K is for...
K is for Kelly. (Mrs. Keyes)
K is for Kevin. (Barbara)
K is for kite. (William)
K is for kitten. (Katie)
K is for keys. (Jeffrey)

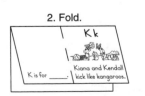

K is for kitten. (Katie)

K is for...

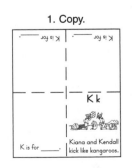

1. Copy.

K is for _____ Kiana and Kendall kick like kangaroos.

2. Fold.

3. Take home.

34

L l

Larry and Linda lick lemon lollipops.

Day 1

Read the tongue twister to the class and:
- ask the children to listen for words that start alike
- ask the children to look at the letter that begins those words..........**L l**
- ask for names that begin with that letter and sound
  - **Lisa, Louis, Lindsay, Lorenzo, LaDonna**
- ask for other words that begin with the same sound
  - **little, left, lamp, light**

Begin a predictable chart by modeling the first sentence, then have the children dictate sentences of their own.

Day 2

Have the rest of the children dictate their sentences.

Day 3

Have each child touch read his sentence.

Day 4

Cut the chart into strips and give each child his strip. Have each child cut his strip into words, reassemble and glue it on a large piece of paper, and then illustrate it.

Day 5

The children's completed papers are combined into a class book, and children make take-home books of the letter.

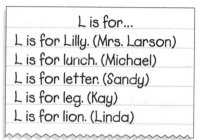

L is for...
L is for Lilly. (Mrs. Larson)
L is for lunch. (Michael)
L is for letter. (Sandy)
L is for leg. (Kay)
L is for lion. (Linda)

L is for lion. (Linda)

L is for...

1. Copy.

L is for _____   Linda and Larry lick lemon lollipops.

2. Fold.

3. Take home.

M m

Marcus and Michelle munch marshmallows.

Day 1

Read the tongue twister to the class and:
- ask the children to listen for words that start alike
- ask the children to look at the letter that begins those words...........**M m**
- ask for names that begin with that letter and sound
  - **Michael, Mandy, Manuel, Madeline, Marika**
- ask for other words that begin with the same sound
  - **me, mother, man, Monday**

Begin a predictable chart by modeling the first sentence, then have the children dictate sentences of their own.

Day 2

Have the rest of the children dictate their sentences.

Day 3

Have each child touch read her sentence.

Day 4

Cut the chart into strips and give each child her strip. Have each child cut her strip into words, reassemble and glue it on a large piece of paper, and then illustrate it.

Day 5

The children's completed papers are combined into a class book, and children make take-home books of the letter.

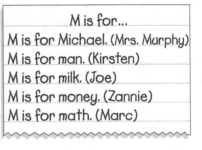

M is for...
M is for Michael. (Mrs. Murphy)
M is for man. (Kirsten)
M is for milk. (Joe)
M is for money. (Zannie)
M is for math. (Marc)

M is for man. (Kirsten)

M is for...

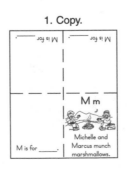

1. Copy.

M is for _____

Michelle and Marcus munch marshmallows.

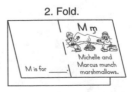

2. Fold.

3. Take home.

N n

Nick and Natasha nibble nuts.

Day 1

Read the tongue twister to the class and:

- ask the children to listen for words that start alike
- ask the children to look at the letter that begins those words...........**N n**
- ask for names that begin with that letter and sound
  - **Nancy, Neal, Nellie, Nathan, Natrone**
- ask for other words that begin with the same sound
  - **no, night, noon, nine**

Begin a predictable chart by modeling the first sentence, then have the children dictate sentences of their own.

Day 2

Have the rest of the children dictate their sentences.

Day 3

Have each child touch read his sentence.

Day 4

Cut the chart into strips and give each child his strip. Have each child cut his strip into words, reassemble and glue it on a large piece of paper, and then illustrate it.

Day 5

The children's completed papers are combined into a class book, and children make take-home books of the letter.

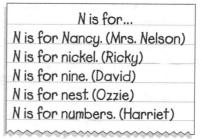

N is for...
N is for Nancy. (Mrs. Nelson)
N is for nickel. (Ricky)
N is for nine. (David)
N is for nest. (Ozzie)
N is for numbers. (Harriet)

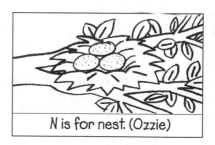

N is for nest. (Ozzie)

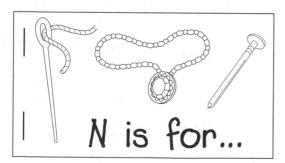

N is for...

1. Copy.

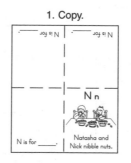

2. Fold.

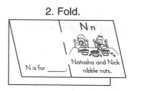

3. Take home.

O o

Omar and Owen open oatmeal boxes.

Day 1

Read the tongue twister to the class and:
- ask the children to listen for words that start alike
- ask the children to look at the letter that begins those words...........**O o**
- ask for names that begin with that letter and sound
  - **Ophelia, Otis, Opal, Olivia**
- ask for other words that begin with the same sound
  - **ocean, oboe, open, over**

Begin a predictable chart by modeling the first sentence, then have the children dictate sentences of their own.

Day 2

Have the rest of the children dictate their sentences.

Day 3

Have each child touch read her sentence.

Day 4

Cut the chart into strips and give each child her strip. Have each child cut her strip into words, reassemble and glue it on a large piece of paper, and then illustrate it.

Day 5

The children's completed papers are combined into a class book, and children make take-home books of the letter.

O is for...
O is for Omar. (Ms. O'Dell)
O is for oatmeal. (Janice)
O is for ocean. (Michael)
O is for oak. (Robbie)
O is for okra. (Reid)

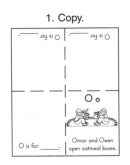

O is for oak. (Robbie)

O is for...

1. Copy.

2. Fold.

3. Take home.

Ollie orders orange juice and an omelet.

Day 1

Read the tongue twister to the class and:
- ask the children to listen for words that start alike
- ask the children to look at the letter that begins those words..........**O o**
- ask for names that begin with that letter and sound
  - **Oscar, Olive, Otto, Oriana, Ozzie**
- ask for other words that begin with the same sound
  - **olive, orange, on**

Begin a predictable chart by modeling the first sentence, then have the children dictate sentences of their own.

Day 2

Have the rest of the children dictate their sentences.

Day 3

Have each child touch read his sentence.

Day 4

Cut the chart into strips and give each child his strip. Have each child cut his strip into words, reassemble and glue it on a large piece of paper, and then illustrate it.

Day 5

The children's completed papers are combined into a class book, and children make take-home books of the letter.

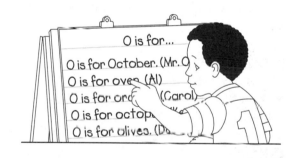

O is for...
O is for October. (Mr. Ontrop)
O is for oven. (Al)
O is for orange. (Carol)
O is for octopus. (Kevin)
O is for olives. (David)

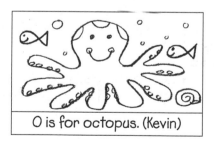

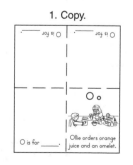

O is for octopus. (Kevin)

O is for...

1. Copy.

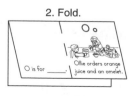

2. Fold.

3. Take home.

P p

Pat and Paul pick pickles and peppers.

Day 1

Read the tongue twister to the class and:
- ask the children to listen for words that start alike
- ask the children to look at the letter that begins those words..........**P p**
- ask for names that begin with that letter and sound
  - **Pamela, Patrick, Priscilla, Peter, Pablo**
- ask for other words that begin with the same sound
  - **paper, pull, pan, present**

Begin a predictable chart by modeling the first sentence, then have the children dictate sentences of their own.

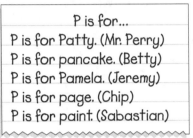

P is for...
P is for Patty. (Mr. Perry)
P is for pancake. (Betty)
P is for Pamela. (Jeremy)
P is for page. (Chip)
P is for paint. (Sabastian)

Day 2

Have the rest of the children dictate their sentences.

Day 3

Have each child touch read her sentence.

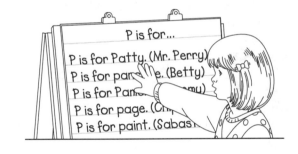

Day 4

Cut the chart into strips and give each child her strip. Have each child cut her strip into words, reassemble and glue it on a large piece of paper, and then illustrate it.

Day 5

The children's completed papers are combined into a class book, and children make take-home books of the letter.

P is for pancake. (Betty)

P is for...

1. Copy.

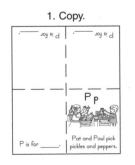

2. Fold.

3. Take home.

40

Q q

Quinton and Queenie quilt quickly and quietly.

Day 1

Read the tongue twister to the class and:
- ask the children to listen for words that start alike
- ask the children to look at the letter that begins those words..........**Q q**
- ask for names that begin with that letter and sound
  - **Queenie, Quanterius, Quincy**
- ask for other words that begin with the same sound
  - **queen, quiet, quiz, question**

Begin a predictable chart by modeling the first sentence, then have the children dictate sentences of their own.

Day 2

Have the rest of the children dictate their sentences.

Day 3

Have each child touch read his sentence.

Day 4

Cut the chart into strips and give each child his strip. Have each child cut his strip into words, reassemble and glue it on a large piece of paper, and then illustrate it.

Day 5

The children's completed papers are combined into a class book, and children make take-home books of the letter.

Q is for...
Q is for Quinton. (Mrs. Quinn)
Q is for quarter. (Marcus)
Q is for queen. (Lisa)
Q is for quilt. (Katherine)
Q is for question. (Cheri)

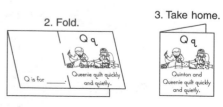

Q is for quarter. (Marcia)

Q is for...

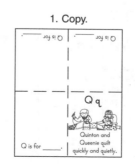

1. Copy.

2. Fold.

3. Take home.

41

R r

Ralph and Ramona rest and read.

Day 1

Read the tongue twister to the class and:
- ask the children to listen for words that start alike
- ask the children to look at the letter that begins those words...........**R r**
- ask for names that begin with that letter and sound
  - **Randall, Renita, Ray, Regina, Rosemary**
- ask for other words that begin with the same sound
  - **run, read, rat, rock, room**

Begin a predictable chart by modeling the first sentence, then have the children dictate sentences of their own.

Day 2

Have the rest of the children dictate their sentences.

Day 3

Have each child touch read her sentence.

Day 4

Cut the chart into strips and give each child her strip. Have each child cut her strip into words, reassemble and glue it on a large piece of paper, and then illustrate it.

Day 5

The children's completed papers are combined into a class book, and children make take-home books of the letter.

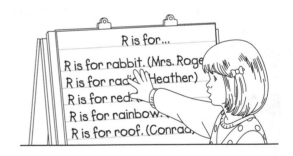

R is for...
R is for rabbit. (Mrs. Rogers)
R is for radio. (Heather)
R is for red. (Bob)
R is for rainbow. (Ashley)
R is for roof. (Conrad)

R is for...
R is for rabbit. (Mrs. Roge
R is for radio. (Heather)
R is for red.
R is for rainbow.
R is for roof. (Conrad)

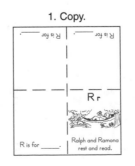

R is for rainbow. (Ashley)

R is for...

1. Copy.

2. Fold.

R r

R is for _____

Ralph and Ramona rest and read.

3. Take home.

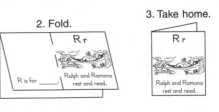

R r

Ralph and Ramona rest and read.

S s

Suzanne and Sammy sail at the seashore.

Day 1

Read the tongue twister to the class and:
- ask the children to listen for words that start alike
- ask the children to look at the letter that begins those words..........**S s**
- ask for names that begin with that letter and sound
  - **Suzanne, Steve, Sabena, Scott, Seth**
- ask for other words that begin with the same sound
  - **six, sea, sun, soup**

Begin a predictable chart by modeling the first sentence, then have the children dictate sentences of their own.

Day 2

Have the rest of the children dictate their sentences.

Day 3

Have each child touch read his sentence.

Day 4

Cut the chart into strips and give each child his strip. Have each child cut his strip into words, reassemble and glue it on a large piece of paper, and then illustrate it.

Day 5

The children's completed papers are combined into a class book, and children make take-home books of the letter.

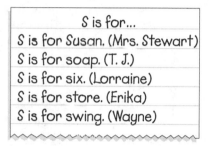

S is for...
S is for Susan. (Mrs. Stewart)
S is for soap. (T. J.)
S is for six. (Lorraine)
S is for store. (Erika)
S is for swing. (Wayne)

S is for swing. (Wayne)

S is for...

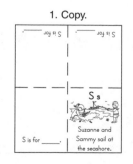

1. Copy.

S is for ___.

2. Fold.

S is for ___.

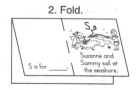

3. Take home.

Sh sh

Shandra shops for shoes and shampoo.

Day 1

Read the tongue twister to the class and:
- ask the children to listen for words that start alike
- ask the children to look at the letters that begin those words...........**Sh sh**
- ask for names that begin with the letters and sound
  - **Shannon, Shelley, Shaquille, Shaun, Shelby**
- ask for other words that begin with the same sound
  - **shell, ship, show, shade, she**

Begin a predictable chart by modeling the first sentence, then have the children dictate sentences of their own.

Sh is for...
Sh is for ship. (Mrs. Sharples)
Sh is for shoe. (Anne)
Sh is for shower. (Eddie)
Sh is for shape. (Mary)
Sh is for shark. (Rashid)

Day 2

Have the rest of the children dictate their sentences.

Day 3

Have each child touch read her sentence.

Day 4

Cut the chart into strips and give each child her strip. Have each child cut her strip into words, reassemble and glue it on a large piece of paper, and then illustrate it.

Day 5

The children's completed papers are combined into a class book, and children make take-home books of the sound.

Sh is for shell. (Tracy)

Sh is for...

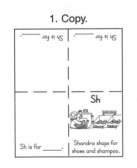

1. Copy.

Sh is for _____

Sh

Shandra shops for shoes and shampoo.

2. Fold.

Sh

Sh is for _____

Shandra shops for shoes and shampoo.

3. Take home.

Sh

Shandra shops for shoes and shampoo.

T t

Tori tells Tommy about tacos and tomatoes.

Day 1

Read the tongue twister to the class and:
- ask the children to listen for words that start alike
- ask the children to look at the letter that begins those words...........**T t**
- ask for names that begin with that letter and sound
  - **Tara, Tim, Tonya, Tyler, Tracy**
- ask for other words that begin with the same sound
  - **two, tent, table, talk, today**

Begin a predictable chart by modeling the first sentence, then have the children dictate sentences of their own.

Day 2

Have the rest of the children dictate their sentences.

Day 3

Have each child touch read his sentence.

Day 4

Cut the chart into strips and give each child his strip. Have each child cut his strip into words, reassemble and glue it on a large piece of paper, and then illustrate it.

Day 5

The children's completed papers are combined into a class book, and children make take-home books of the letter.

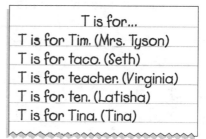

T is for...
T is for Tim. (Mrs. Tyson)
T is for taco. (Seth)
T is for teacher. (Virginia)
T is for ten. (Latisha)
T is for Tina. (Tina)

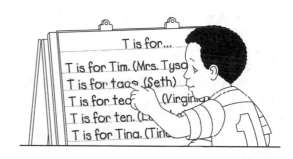

T is for teacher. (Virginia)

T is for...

1. Copy.

2. Fold.

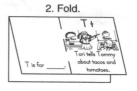

3. Take home.

Th th

Thelma thanks Thad for the thimble.

Day 1

Read the tongue twister to the class and:
- ask the children to listen for words that start alike
- ask the children to look at the letters that begin those words...........**Th th**
- ask for names that begin with the letters and sound
  - **Thelma, Thad, Theodore**
- ask for other words that begin with the same sound
  - **thumb, three, thing, thunder**

Begin a predictable chart by modeling the first sentence, then have the children dictate sentences of their own.

Day 2

Have the rest of the children dictate their sentences.

Day 3

Have each child touch read her sentence.

Day 4

Cut the chart into strips and give each child her strip. Have each child cut her strip into words, reassemble and glue it on a large piece of paper, and then illustrate it.

Day 5

The children's completed papers are combined into a class book, and children make take-home books of the sound.

Th is for...
Th is for thin. (Mr. Thorn)
Th is for thread. (Megan)
Th is for thank. (Rob)
Th is for three. (Sean)
Th is for thermos. (Owen)

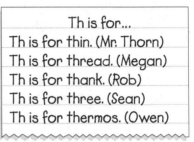

Th is for thermos. (Owen)

Th is for...

1. Copy.

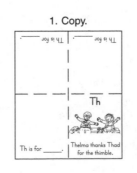

2. Fold.

3. Take home.

U u

Ulysses's Unicorn

Ulysses has a unicorn and a ukulele.

Day 1

Read the tongue twister to the class and:
- ask the children to listen for words that start alike
- ask the children to look at the letter that begins those words...........**U u**
- ask for names that begin with that letter and sound
  - **Ulysses, Uriah**
- ask for other words that begin with the same sound
  - **United States, Utah, unicorn**

Begin a predictable chart by modeling the first sentence, then have the children dictate sentences of their own.

Day 2

Have the rest of the children dictate their sentences.

Day 3

Have each child touch read her sentence.

Day 4

Cut the chart into strips and give each child her strip. Have each child cut her strip into words, reassemble and glue it on a large piece of paper, and then illustrate it.

Day 5

The children's completed papers are combined into a class book, and children make take-home books of the letter.

U is for...
U is for unicorn. (Mr. Bell)
U is for unit. (Pamela)
U is for Unifix® cube. (Taylor)
U is for universe. (Marty)
U is for unicycle. (Maurice)

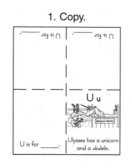

U is for unicycle. (Maurice)

U is for ...

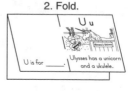

1. Copy.

2. Fold.

3. Take home.

U u

Ursula's uncle stays under an umbrella.

Day 1

Read the tongue twister to the class and:
- ask the children to listen for words that start alike
- ask the children to look at the letter that begins those words...........**U u**
- ask for names that begin with that letter and sound
  - **Ursula, Upton, Ulric**
- ask for other words that begin with the same sound
  - **umbrella, ugly, up, under, us**

Begin a predictable chart by modeling the first sentence, then have the children dictate sentences of their own.

Day 2

Have the rest of the children dictate their sentences.

Day 3

Have each child touch read his sentence.

Day 4

Cut the chart into strips and give each child his strip. Have each child cut his strip into words, reassemble and glue it on a large piece of paper, and then illustrate it.

Day 5

The children's completed papers are combined into a class book, and children make take-home books of the letter.

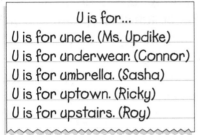

U is for...
U is for uncle. (Ms. Updike)
U is for underwear. (Connor)
U is for umbrella. (Sasha)
U is for uptown. (Ricky)
U is for upstairs. (Roy)

U is for umbrella. (Sasha)

I U is for...

1. Copy.

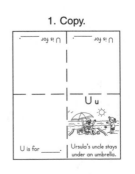

2. Fold.

3. Take home.

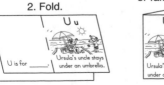

48

V v

Vincent visits Vickie to view a video.

Day 1

Read the tongue twister to the class and:
- ask the children to listen for words that start alike
- ask the children to look at the letter that begins those words...........**V v**
- ask for names that begin with that letter and sound
  - **Vernon, Violet, Virgil, Venus, Virginia**
- ask for other words that begin with the same sound
  - **van, vase, video, vest**

Begin a predictable chart by modeling the first sentence, then have the children dictate sentences of their own.

Day 2

Have the rest of the children dictate their sentences.

Day 3

Have each child touch read his sentence.

Day 4

Cut the chart into strips and give each child his strip. Have each child cut his strip into words, reassemble and glue it on a large piece of paper, and then illustrate it.

Day 5

The children's completed papers are combined into a class book, and children make take-home books of the letter.

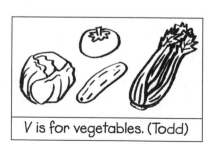

V is for...
V is for Violet. (Mrs. Velspar)
V is for vegetables. (Todd)
V is for vanilla. (Evelyn)
V is for vet. (Wade)
V is for video. (Joanna)

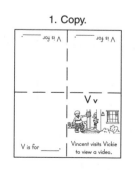

V is for vegetables. (Todd)

V is for...

1. Copy.

2. Fold.

3. Take home.

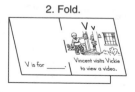

W w

William and Wendy wiggle like worms.

Day 1

Read the tongue twister to the class and:
- ask the children to listen for words that start alike
- ask the children to look at the letter that begins those words...........**W w**
- ask for names that begin with that letter and sound
  - **Wanda, Wesley, Whitney, Winifred, Wayne**
- ask for other words that begin with the same sound
  - **watermelon, waiter, we, weather**

Begin a predictable chart by modeling the first sentence, then have the children dictate sentences of their own.

Day 2

Have the rest of the children dictate their sentences.

Day 3

Have each child touch read her sentence.

Day 4

Cut the chart into strips and give each child her strip. Have each child cut her strip into words, reassemble and glue it on a large piece of paper, and then illustrate it.

Day 5

The children's completed papers are combined into a class book, and children make take-home books of the letter.

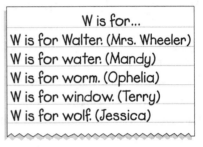

W is for...
W is for Walter. (Mrs. Wheeler)
W is for water. (Mandy)
W is for worm. (Ophelia)
W is for window. (Terry)
W is for wolf. (Jessica)

W is for window. (Terry)

W is for...

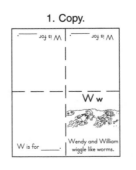

1. Copy.

2. Fold.

3. Take home.

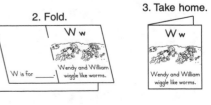

 X x

Xavier put x's on the x-ray.

Day 1

Read the tongue twister to the class and:
- ask the children to listen for words that start alike
- ask the children to look at the letter that begins those words..........**X x**
- ask for names that begin with that letter and sound(s)
  - **Xavier, Xenia, Xandra**
- ask for other words that have the same sound(s)
  - **xylophone, x-ray, box**

Begin a predictable chart by modeling the first sentence, then have the children dictate sentences of their own.

Day 2

Have the rest of the children dictate their sentences.

Day 3

Have each child touch read his sentence.

Day 4

Cut the chart into strips and give each child his strip. Have each child cut his strip into words, reassemble and glue it on a large piece of paper, and then illustrate it.

Day 5

The children's completed papers are combined into a class book, and children make take-home books of the letter.

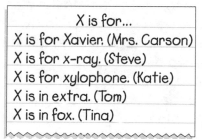

X is for...
X is for Xavier. (Mrs. Carson)
X is for x-ray. (Steve)
X is for xylophone. (Katie)
X is in extra. (Tom)
X is in fox. (Tina)

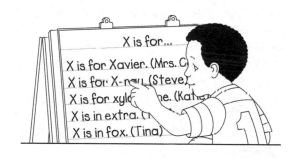

X is in fox. (Tina)

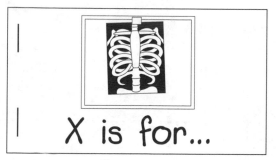

X is for...

1. Copy.

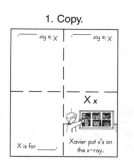

2. Fold.

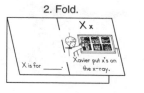

3. Take home.

51

Y y

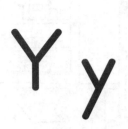

Yolanda and Yasmin yell for yellow yo-yos.

Day 1

Read the tongue twister to the class and:
- ask the children to listen for words that start alike
- ask the children to look at the letter that begins those words...........**Y y**
- ask for names that begin with that letter and sound
  - **Yolanda, Yasir, Yancey**
- ask for other words that begin with the same sound
  - **yogurt, yellow, yes, you**

Begin a predictable chart by modeling the first sentence, then have the children dictate sentences of their own.

Day 2

Have the rest of the children dictate their sentences.

Day 3

Have each child touch read her sentence.

Day 4

Cut the chart into strips and give each child her strip. Have each child cut her strip into words, reassemble and glue it on a large piece of paper, and then illustrate it.

Day 5

The children's completed papers are combined into a class book, and children make take-home books of the letter.

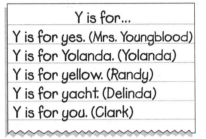

Y is for...
Y is for yes. (Mrs. Youngblood)
Y is for Yolanda. (Yolanda)
Y is for yellow. (Randy)
Y is for yacht. (Delinda)
Y is for you. (Clark)

Y is for yard. (Henry)

Y is for...

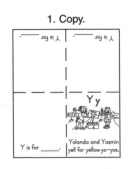

1. Copy.

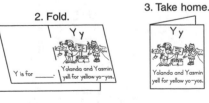

2. Fold.

3. Take home.

Z z

Zach zigzagged through the zoo with Zannie.

Day 1

Read the tongue twister to the class and:
- ask the children to listen for words that start alike
- ask the children to look at the letter that begins those words...........**Z z**
- ask for names that begin with that letter and sound
  - **Zeke, Zoe, Zeno, Zola**
- ask for other words that begin with the same sound
  - **zebra, zero, zoom**

Begin a predictable chart by modeling the first sentence, then have the children dictate sentences of their own.

Day 2

Have the rest of the children dictate their sentences.

Day 3

Have each child touch read his sentence.

Day 4

Cut the chart into strips and give each child his strip. Have each child cut his strip into words, reassemble and glue it on a large piece of paper, and then illustrate it.

Day 5

The children's completed papers are combined into a class book, and children make take-home books of the letter.

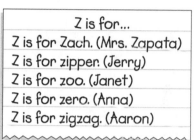

Z is for...
Z is for Zach. (Mrs. Zapata)
Z is for zipper. (Jerry)
Z is for zoo. (Janet)
Z is for zero. (Anna)
Z is for zigzag. (Aaron)

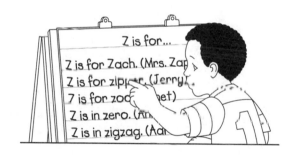

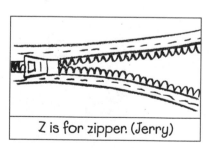

Z is for zipper. (Jerry)

ZOO

Z is for...

1. Copy.

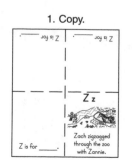

Z is for
Z z
Zach zigzagged through the zoo with Zannie.
Z is for _____.

2. Fold.

3. Take home.

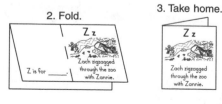

A is for ‾‾‾‾‾‾‾‾‾‾‾‾‾‾ .

A is for ‾‾‾‾‾‾‾‾‾‾‾‾‾‾ .

A a

Amie and Asia ate apricots.

A is for ‾‾‾‾‾‾‾‾‾‾‾‾‾‾ .

54

A is for _____ .

A is for _____ .

A a

Alex and Amber always
avoid asparagus.

A is for _____ .

B is for _____ .

B is for _____ .

B b

Brianna and Ben bounce
beach balls.

B is for _____ .

C is for _____.

C is for _____ (upside down, top right)

C is for _____ (upside down, top left)

C c

Carol and Caitlyn
count candy corn.

C is for _____ .

C is for _____ .

C c

Cindy celebrates with cider and celery.

C is for _____ .

Ch is for _____.

Ch is for _____.

Ch ch

Chad and Chip chew cherries
and chocolate.

Ch is for _____.

D is for _____.

D is for _____.

D d

David and Dominique dance with Dalmatians.

D is for _____.

_____ .

E is for

_____

E is for

E e

Elizabeth and Ethan

eat eclairs.

E is for _____ .

E is for _____.

E is for _____.

E e

Emily and Eddie enjoy eggs.

E is for _____.

F is for _____ .

F is for _____ .

F is for

F f

Felicia and Freddy follow
funny footprints.

G is for _____.

G is for _____.

G g

Gail and Gwen grow goodies
in their garden.

G is for _____.

G is for ⎯⎯⎯⎯⎯⎯⎯ .

G is for ⎯⎯⎯⎯⎯⎯⎯ .

G g

Ginger and George like giraffes and gerbils.

G is for ⎯⎯⎯⎯⎯⎯⎯ .

H is for _____.

H is for _____.

H h

Hannah hugs Harry
the happy hound.

H is for _____.

I is for _____.

I is for _____.

I i

Isaac and Iris like ice cubes and ice cream.

I is for _____.

I is for _____.

I is for _____.

I i

Isadora and Iggie have inchworms that itch.

I is for _____.

J is for _____.

J is for _____.

Jj

Jeremy and Jazmin
jiggle like jelly.

J is for _____.

K is for _____ .

K is for _____ .

K k

Kendall and Kiana
kick like kangaroos.

K is for _____ .

L is for _____ .

L is for _____ .

Ll

Larry and Linda lick
lemon lollipops.

L is for _____ .

M is for _____.

M is for _____.

M m

Marcus and Michelle munch marshmallows.

M is for _____.

N is for ＿＿＿＿＿＿＿＿＿.

N is for ＿＿＿＿＿＿＿＿＿.

N n

Nick and Natasha nibble nuts.

O is for _____ .

O is for _____ .

O o

Omar and Owen open
oatmeal boxes.

O is for _____ .

74

O is for _____.

O is for

O o

Ollie orders orange juice
and an omelet.

O is for _____.

P is for _____.

P is for _____.

P p

Pat and Paul pick pickles
and peppers.

P is for _____.

Q is for _____.

Q is for _____.

Q q

Quinton and Queenie quilt quickly and quietly.

Q is for _____.

R is for _____.

R is for _____.

R r

Ralph and Ramona
rest and read.

R is for _____.

S is for _____.

S is for _____.

S s

Suzanne and Sammy sail at the seashore.

S is for _____.

Sh is for _____ .

Sh is for _____ .

Sh sh

**Shandra shops for
shoes and shampoo.**

Sh is for _____ .

⊤ is for _____ •

⊤ is for _____ •

T t

Tori tells Tommy about tacos and tomatoes.

T is for _____ .

Th is for _____.

Th is for _____.

Th th

Thelma thanks Thad
for the thimble.

Th is for _____.

82

U is for _____.

U is for _____.

U u

Ursula's uncle stays under
an umbrella.

U is for _____.

U is for _____.

U is for _____.

U u

Ulysses's Unicorn

Ulysses has a unicorn
and a ukulele.

U is for _____.

V is for _____.

V is for _____.

Vincent visits Vickie
to view a video.

V is for _____.

W is for _____ .

W is for _____ .

Ww

William and Wendy wiggle
like worms.

W is for _____ .

X is for _____.

X is for _____.

Xavier put x's on the x-ray.

X is for _____.

Y is for _____ .

Y is for _____ .

Y y

Yolanda and Yasmin yell for
yellow yo-yos.

Y is for _____ .

Z is for _____.

Z is for _____.

Z z

Zach zigzagged through the zoo with Zannie.

Z is for _____.

90

References

Professional References

Adams, Marilyn Jager. (1991) *Beginning to Read: Thinking and Learning about Print.* Cambridge, MA: MIT Press.

Cunningham, Patricia M. "Beginning Reading without Readiness: Structural Language Experience." *Reading Horizons.* (Spring 1979): 222-227.

Cunningham, Patricia M. & Allington, Richard L. (2001) *Schools that Work: Where All Children Read and Write.* New York: Addison Wesley Longman.

Cunningham, Patricia M., Hall, Dorothy P., & Sigmon, Cheryl M. (1999) *The Teacher's Guide to the Four-Blocks®.* Greensboro, NC: Carson-Dellosa Publishing, Inc.

Hall, Dorothy P. & Cunningham, Patricia M. (1997) *Month-by-Month Reading and Writing for Kindergarten.* Greensboro, NC: Carson-Dellosa Publishing, Inc.

Hall, Dorothy P. & Williams, Elaine. (2000) *The Teacher's Guide to Building Blocks.* Greensboro, NC: Carson-Dellosa Publishing, Inc.

Hall, Dorothy P. & Williams, Elaine. (2001) *Predictable Charts: Shared Writing for Kindergarten and First Grade.* Greensboro, NC: Carson-Dellosa Publishing, Inc.

Yopp, Hallie Kay. "Developing Phonemic Awareness." *Reading Teacher.* 45, no. 9 (1992).

Children's Works Cited

ABCD: An Alphabet Book of Cats and Dogs by Sheila Moxley (Little Brown Children's Books, 2001).

Animalia by Graeme Base (Harry N. Abrams, Inc., 1993).

Alphabet Books

Alphabet books help young children to learn about letters and sounds. Here is a list of some of my favorite alphabet books. The books with asterisks are more difficult and the vocabulary may not be appropriate for younger students.

Dorothy Hall

A Apple Pie by Kate Greenaway (Derrydale Books, 1993).

A Is for Africa by Ifeoma Onyefulu (Penguin, 1997).

A Is for Animals by David Pelham (Simon & Schuster, 1991).

A Is for Artist: A Getty Museum Alphabet (J. Paul Getty Museum Publications, 1997).

A Is for Asia by Cynthia Chin-Lee (Orchard Books, 1997).

A Is for Astronaut by Sian Tucker (Simon & Schuster, 1995).

A My Name Is Alice by Jane Bayer (Dial Books, 1987).

A to Z by Sandra Boynton (Little Simon, 1995).

A to Z Sticker Book by Jan Pienkowski (Random House, 1995).

A You're Adorable by Buddy Kaye, Fred Wise, & Sidney Lippman (Candlewick Press,1994).

ABC Book by C. B. Falls (William Morrow & Co., 1998).

The ABC Bunny by Wanda Gag (Putnam, 1997).

ABC for You and Me by Meg Girnis (Albert Whitman & Co., 2000).

ABC I Like Me! by Nancy L. Carlson (Penguin, 1999).

ABC T-Rex by Bernard Most (Harcourt, Inc., 2000).

ABCD: An Alphabet Book of Cats and Dogs by Sheila Moxley (Little Brown Children's Books, 2001).

A-Boo-C: A Spooky Alphabet Story by Pamela Jane (Penguin Putnam Books for Young Readers,1998).

The Accidental Zucchini by Max Grover (Harcourt, 1993).

Alaska ABC Book by Charlene Kreeger (Econo-Clad Books, 1999).

Albert's Alphabet by Leslie Tryon (Simon & Schuster, 1991).

Alfabetiere by Renza Zanne (Demetra, 1997).*

All Aboard ABC by Doug McGee & Robert Newman (Dutton Children's Books, 1990).

Alligators All Around: An Alphabet by Maurice Sendak (HarperTrophy, 1990).

Alpha Beta Chowder by Jeanne Steig & William Steig (HarperCollins, 1992).

Alphababies by Kim Golding (Dorling Kindersley Publishing, Inc., 1998).

Alphabatics by Suse MacDonald (Bradbury Press, 1986).

Alphabears: An ABC Book by Kathleen Hague (Henry Holt & Co., Inc., 1984).

Alphabet Bandits: An ABC Book by Marcia Leonard (Troll Communications LLC , 1990).

The Alphabet Book by P. D. Eastman (Random House, 1974).

An Alphabet of Dinosaurs by Peter Dodson (Scholastic, 1995).

Alphabet Book Down in the Garden by Anne Geddes (CEDCO Publishers, 1997).

Alphabet City by Stephen Johnson (Viking, 1995).

The Alphabet Flap Book by John Blackman (Joshua Morris, 1991).

Alphabet Parade by Seymour Chwast (Harcourt Brace, 1991).

Amazon Alphabet by Martin Jordan & Tanis Jordan (Scholastic, 1996).

Animal ABC's by Susan Hood (Troll Associates, 1995).

Animal Alphabet by Bert Kitchen (Penguin Books, 1992).

Animal Parade by Jakki Wood (Scholastic, 1993).

Animalia by Graeme Base (Harry N. Abrams, 1993).

Animals A to Z by David McPhail (Scholastic, 1989).

Annie, Bea, and Chi Chi Dolores: A School Day Alphabet by Donna Maurer (Orchard Books, 1993).

Apricot ABC by Miska Miles (Little Brown & Co., 1969).

Arf! Beg! Catch!: Dogs from A to Z by Henry Horenstein (Cartwheel Books, 1999).

Arizona A to Z by Dorothy Hines Weaver (Northland Publishing, 1992).

The Arizona Alphabet Book by Donna Dee Schmid-Belk (Sunbelt Publishing, Inc., 1989).

Arlene Alda's ABC: What Do You See? by Arlene Alda (Ten Speed Press, 1993).

Arnold Plays Baseball by Patricia Whitehead (Troll Associates, 1985).

Ashanti to Zulu: African Traditions by Margaret W. Musgrove (Dial Books for Young Readers, 1992).

Aster Aardvark's Alphabet Adventures by Steven Kellogg (Econo-Clad Books, 1999).

Basketball ABC: The NBA Alphabet by Florence Cassen Mayers (Harry N. Abrams, 1996).

The Bird Alphabet Book by Jerry Pallotta (Charlesbridge Publishing, 1989).*

Black and White Rabbit's ABC by Alan Baker (Larousse Kingfisher Chambers, 1999).

Bob and Larry's ABC's by Phil Vischer (Tommy Nelson, 1997).

The Book of Shadowboxes: A Story of the ABC's by Laura Seeley (Peachtree Publishers, 1994).

Bugs and Beasties ABC by Cheryl Nathan (BookWorld Services, Inc., 1995).

By the Sea: An Alphabet Book by Ann Blades (Kids Can Press, 1985).

Chicka Chicka Boom Boom by Bill Martin, Jr. & John Archambault (Simon & Schuster, 1989).

Children from Australia to Zimbabwe by Maya Ajmera & Anna Rhesa Versola (Charlesbridge Publishing, 1997).

The Christmas Alphabet by Robert Sabuda (Orchard Books, 1994).

Christmas Alphabet Book (ABC Adventure) by Patricia Whitehead (Troll Associates, 1986).

Clifford's ABC by Norman Bridwell (Scholastic, 1990).

A Colonial Williamsburg ABC by Amy Z. Watson (Colonial Williamsburg Foundation, 1994).

Curious George Learns the Alphabet by H. A. Rey (Houghton Mifflin Co., 1963).

Demi's Find the Animal A-B-C by Demi (Putnam Publishing Group, 1985).

Disney's Winnie the Pooh's A to Zzz by Don Ferguson (Scholastic, 1992).

Dr. Seuss's ABC by Dr. Seuss (Random House, 1963).

Eating the Alphabet: Fruits & Vegetables from A to Z by Lois Ehlert (Harcourt Brace, 1989).

The Extinct Alphabet Book by Jerry Pallotta (Charlesbridge Publishing, 1993).*

Farm Alphabet Book by Jane Miller (Econo-Clad Books, 1999).

F-Freezing ABC by Posy Simmonds (Alfred A. Knopf, Inc., 1995).

A Fly in the Sky by Kristin Joy Pratt (Dawn Publications, 1996).

The Frog Alphabet Book by Jerry Pallotta (Charlesbridge Publishing, 1990).*

From Acorn to Zoo and Everything in Between in Alphabetical Order by Satoshi Kitamura (Sunburst, 1992).

From Apple to Zipper by Nora Cohen (Simon & Schuster's Children's, 1993).

From Letter to Letter by Teri Sloat (Puffin Books, 1989).

Halloween ABC by Eve Merriam (Aladdin, 1995).

Harold's ABC by Crockett Johnson (HarperCollins Juvenile Books, 1981).

Here Comes Hungry Albert (ABC Adventure) by Patricia Whitehead (Troll Associates, 1986).

Hieroglyphs from A-Z: A Rhyming Book with Ancient Egyptian Stencils for Kids by Peter DerManuelian (Scholastic, 1991).*

I Spy: An Alphabet in Art by Lucy Mickletwatt (Mulberry Books, 1996).

The Icky Bug Alphabet Book by Jerry Pallota (Charlesbridge Publishing, 1993).*

It Begins with an A by Stephanie Calmenson (Scholastic, 1993).

Jambo Means Hello: Swahili Alphabet Book by Muriel Feelings (Dial Books for Young Readers, 1992).

A Jewish Holiday ABC by Malka Drucker (Voyager Books, 1992).

John Burlingham's ABC by John Burlingham (Crown Publishers, 1964).

K Is for Kiss Goodnight: Bedtime ABC by Jill Sardegna (Delacorte Press, 1994).

Kids Celebrate the Alphabet by Jean Warren (Warren Publishing, 1996).

The Letters are Lost by Lisa Campbell Ernst (Puffin, 1999).

Miss Bindergarten Gets Ready for Kindergarten by Joseph Slate (Puffin, 2001).

Miss Spider's ABC by David Kirk (Scholastic, 2000).

The Monster Book of ABC Sounds by Alan Snow (Penguin Books, 1991).

Navajo ABC: A Diné Alphabet Book by Luci Tapahonso (Aladdin Paperbacks, 1999).

NBA Action from A to Z by James Preller (Scholastic, 1997).

New Mexico A to Z by Dorothy Hines Weaver (Northland Publishing, 1996).

Paddington's ABC by Michael Bond (Puffin, 1996).

Peter Rabbit's ABC by Beatrix Potter (Viking Press, 1987).

Quilt Alphabet by Lesa Cline-Ransome (Holiday House, 2001).

Richard Scarry's Find Your ABC's by Richard Scarry (Random House, 1973).

Sign Language ABC by Linda Bove (Random House, 1985).

The Sweet and Sour Animal Book by Langston Hughes (Oxford University Press Children's Books, 1997).

A *Swim through the Sea* by Kristin Joy Pratt (Dawn Publications, 1994).

Thomas's ABC Book by Wilbert Vere Audry (Random House, 1998).

Tomorrow's Alphabet by George Shannon (Mulberry Books, 1999).

Under the Sea from A to Z by Anne Doubilet (Crown Publishing, 1991).

The Underwater Alphabet Book by Jerry Pallotta (Charlesbridge Publishing, 1991).*

What a Funny Bunny (ABC Adventure) by Patricia Whitehead (Troll Associates, 1985).

The Yucky Reptile Alphabet Book by Jerry Pallotta (Charlesbridge Publishing, 1989).*

Z is for Zombie by Merrily Kutner (Albert Whitman & Co., 1999).

The Z was Zapped: A Play in Twenty-Six Acts by Chris Van Allsburg (Houghton Mifflin, 1987).

Zoophabets by Robert Tallon (Scholastic, 1979).

Notes